Saving Hoppo

Story by Dawn McMillan

Illustrations by Claire Bridge

Hoppo was Ben's little brown rabbit.

She lived outside in a cage,
on the grass.

2

Every morning,
Ben put new straw in Hoppo's house.
He pulled some carrots
out of the garden
for Hoppo's breakfast.

Ben liked to watch Hoppo
nibble the carrots.

After school,
Ben played with Hoppo.
He talked to her and patted her.
Then he put her back into the cage
for the night.

One night it started to rain.
It rained all night long.
It was still raining in the morning
when Dad went to work.

Ben woke up and looked outside.
There was water all over the grass.

"Mom!" shouted Ben.
"There's a flood outside.
The water is going in Hoppo's cage!
She will be all wet and cold
and she will be scared, too."

Mom ran to the window.
"Oh, dear!" she said.
"We will have to move the cage."

"Quick! We have to save Hoppo!"
cried Ben.

Ben and Mom got dressed
in a hurry.
They went outside.

"We are coming, Hoppo!"
called Ben.

Ben ran to Hoppo's cage.
The water was just coming
in the door of her house.
Ben tried to move the cage,
but it was too heavy.

"Wait, Ben!" called Mom.
"I'll pull the cage."

"I'll take Hoppo out first," said Ben.
"Then she won't be scared
when you move the cage."

Ben picked Hoppo up
and held her in his arms.
He patted her.

Mom pulled the cage out of the water.
She pulled it across the grass
and up to the big tree.

Ben put Hoppo back in her cage.
"Now you will be safe," he said.

Ben looked at Hoppo's wet house.
"I'll get you some dry straw,"
he said to her.

"And I'll get her some breakfast,"
said Mom.

"This is a better place
for Hoppo's cage," said Ben.
"Now Hoppo won't get wet
every time it rains."